Editor
Janet Cain, M. Ed.

Managing Editor
Ina Massler Levin, M.A.

Editor-in-Chief
Sharon Coan, M.S. Ed.

Illustrator
Ken Tunell

Cover Artist
Barb Lorseyedi

Art Coordinator
Kevin Barnes

Art Director
CJae Froshay

Imaging
Alfred Lau
Temo Parra

Product Manager
Phil Garcia

Publishers
Rachelle Cracchiolo, M.S. Ed.
Mary Dupuy Smith, M.S. Ed.

Practice Makes Perfect

Traditional Printing

Author

Teacher Created Materials Staff

Teacher Created Materials

Teacher Created Materials, Inc.
6421 Industry Way
Westminster, CA 92683
www.teachercreated.com

©2002 Teacher Created Materials, Inc.
Made in the USA
ISBN-0-7439-3330-3

Table of Contents

Introduction

The old adage "practice makes perfect" can really hold true for your child and his or her education. The more practice and exposure your child has with concepts being taught in school, the more success he or she is likely to find. For many parents, knowing how to help their children may be frustrating because the resources may not be readily available.

As a parent it is also difficult to know where to focus your efforts so that the extra practice your child receives at home supports what he or she is learning in school.

This book has been written to help parents and teachers reinforce basic skills with children. *Practice Makes Perfect: Traditional Printing* helps children learn to correctly form the uppercase and lowercase form of each letter. The exercises in this book can be done sequentially or can be taken out of order, as needed.

The following standards or objectives will be met or reinforced by completing the practice pages included in this book. These standards and objectives are similar to the ones required by your state and school district.

- The student will demonstrate competence in writing the correct form of each uppercase and lowercase letter.
- The student will demonstrate competence in pencil grip and paper position.
- The student will demonstrate competence in writing from left-to-right and top-to-bottom on the page.
- The student will demonstrate competence in writing words legibly in modern printing, using correct letter formation, appropriate size, and spacing.

How to Make the Most of This Book

Here are some useful ideas for making the most of this book:

- Set aside a specific place in your home to work on this book. Keep it neat and tidy with materials ready on hand.
- Set up a certain time of day to work on these practice pages to establish consistency, or look for times in your day or week that are less hectic and conducive to practicing skills.
- Keep all practice sessions with your child positive and constructive. If the mood becomes frustrated or tense, set the book aside and look for another time to practice with your child. Forcing your child to perform will not help. Do not use this book as a punishment.
- Help beginning readers with instructions.
- Review the work your child has done.
- Pay attention to the areas in which your child has the most difficulty. Provide extra guidance and exercises in those areas.
- Look for ways to make real-life application to the skills being reinforced. Play games such as having your child write word lists with you.

The Alphabet

Straight and Slanted Lines, Ovals and Circles

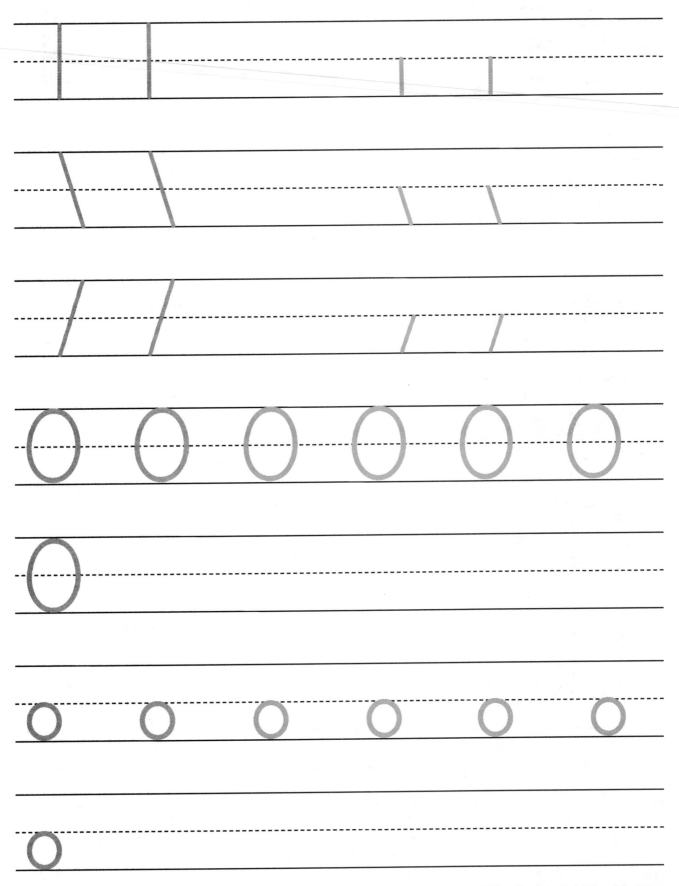

Curves

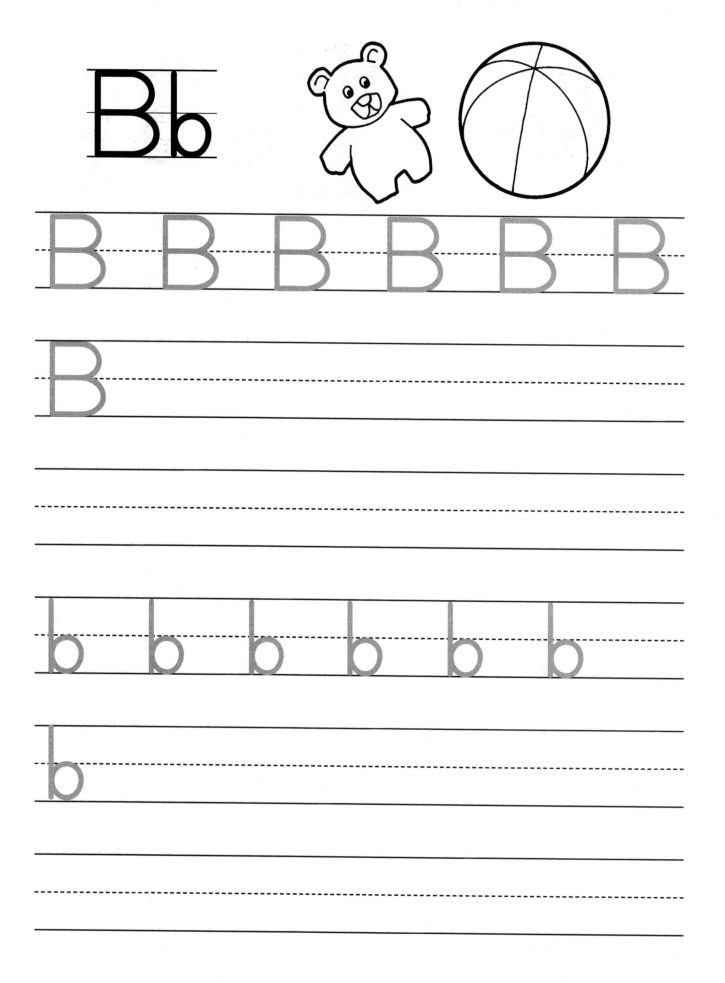

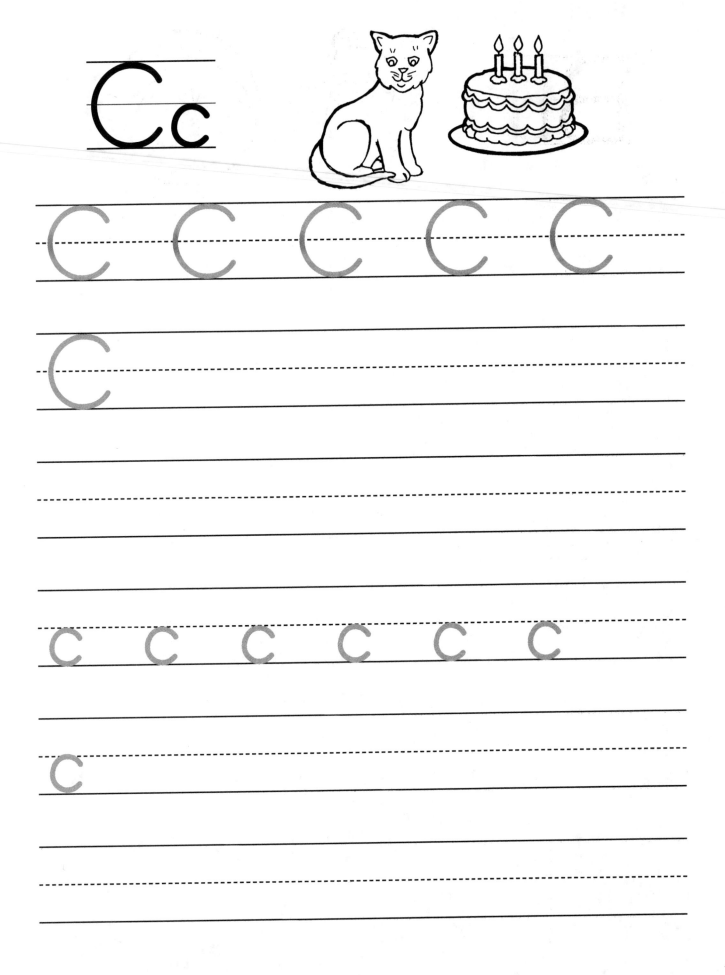

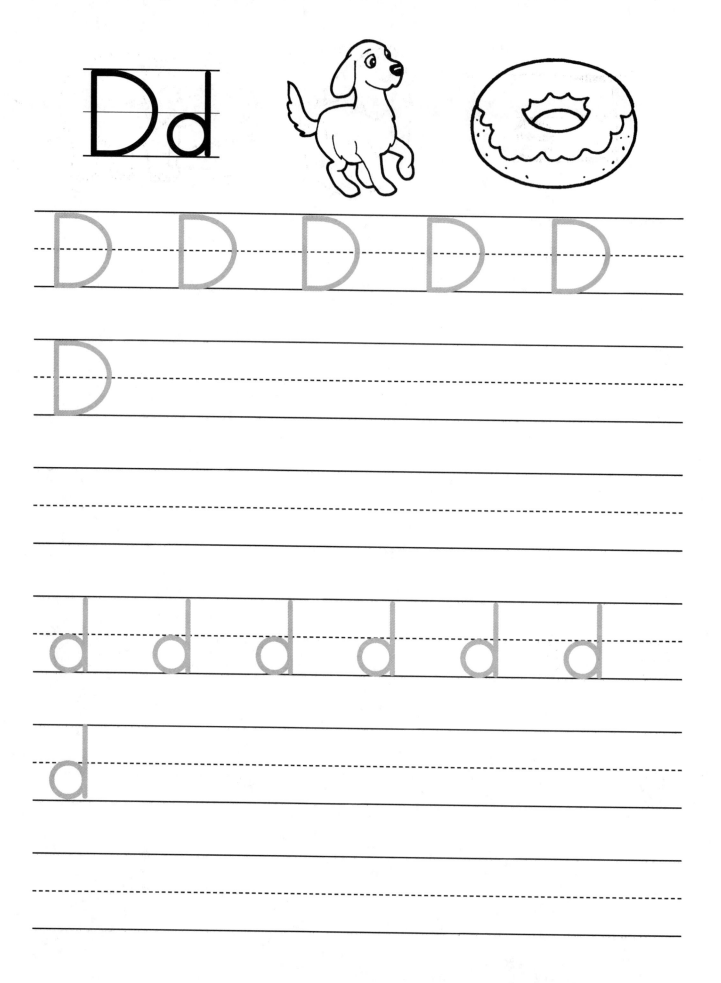

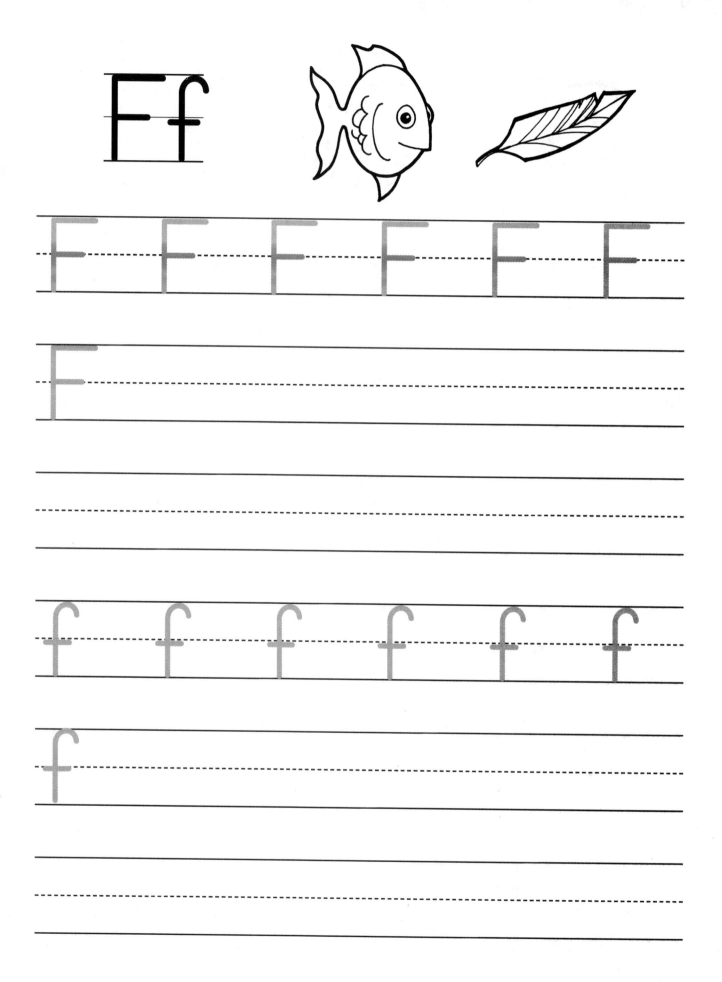

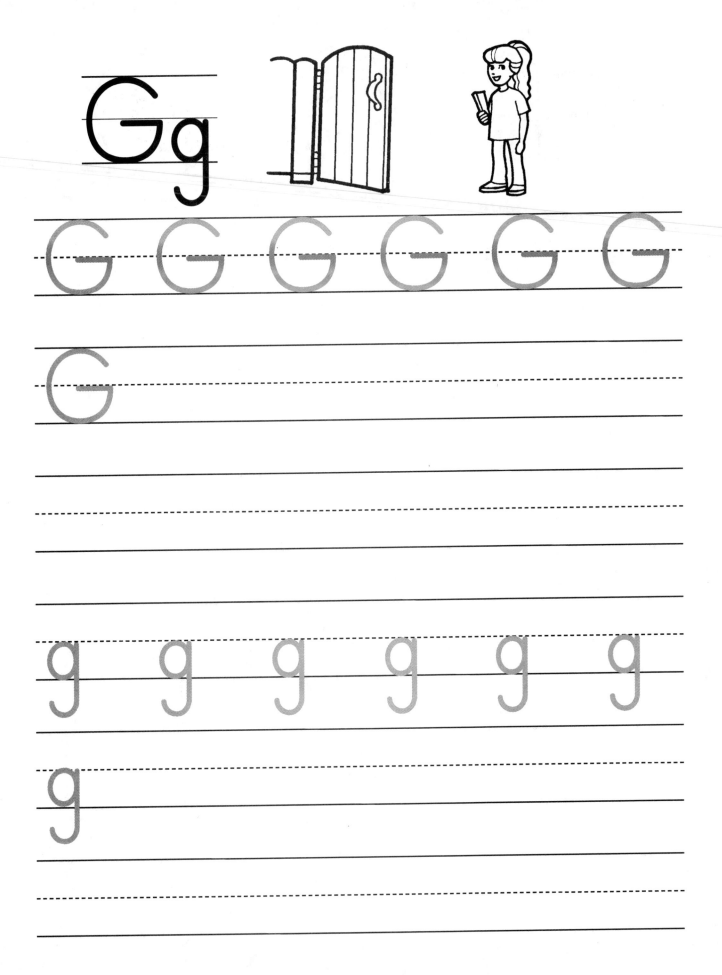

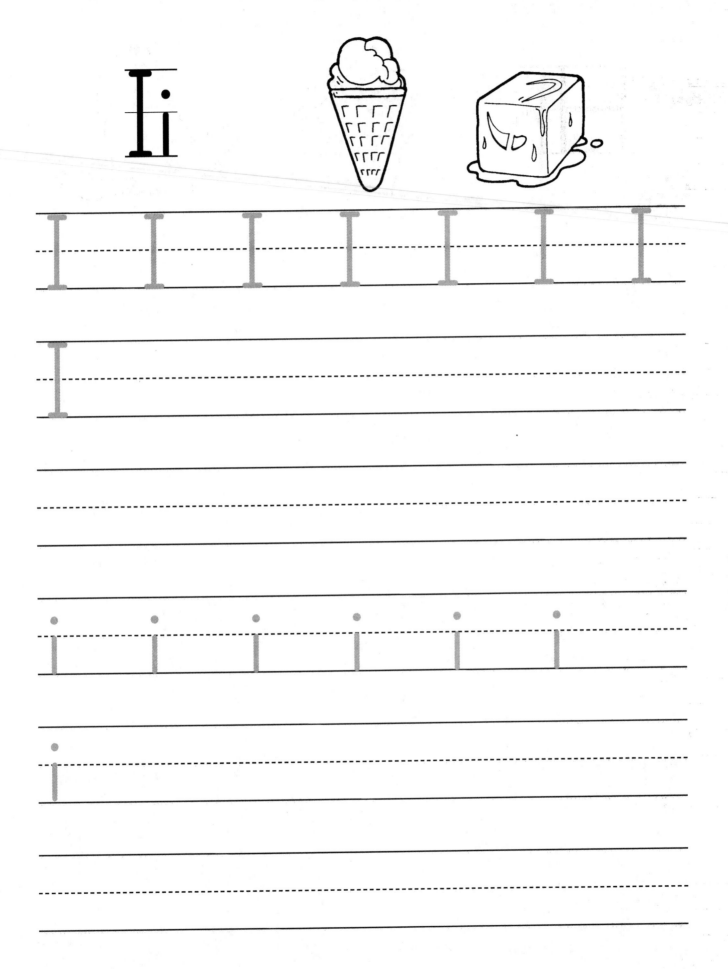

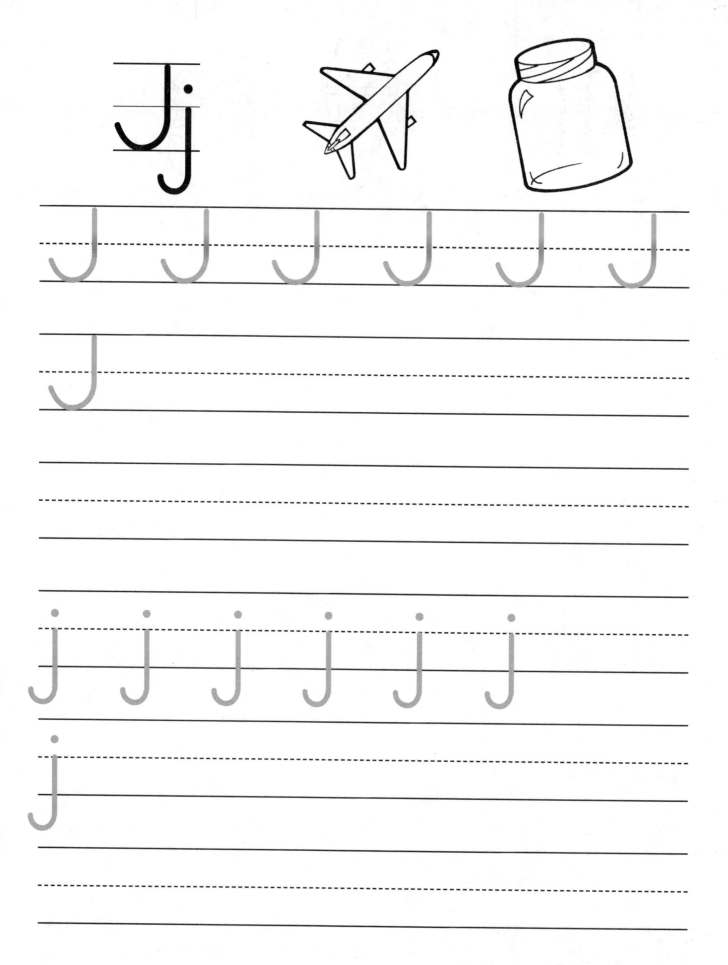

Mm

M M M M M

M

m m m m m

m

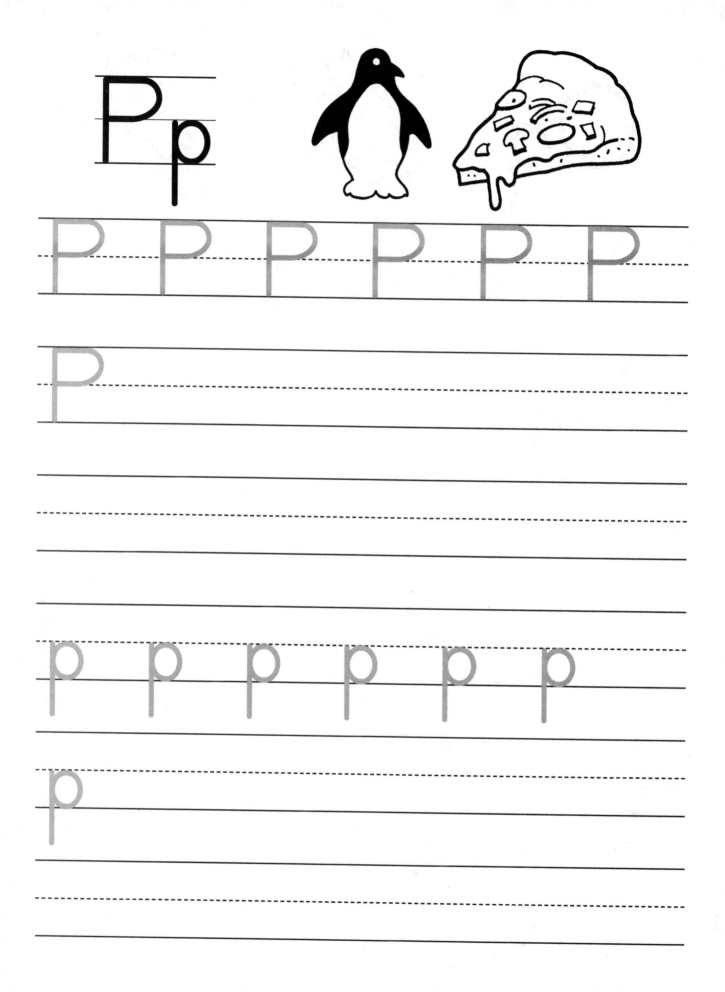

P p

P P P P P P

P

p p p p p p

p

R R R R R

R

r r r r r r

r

Ss

S S S S S S

S

S S S S S

S

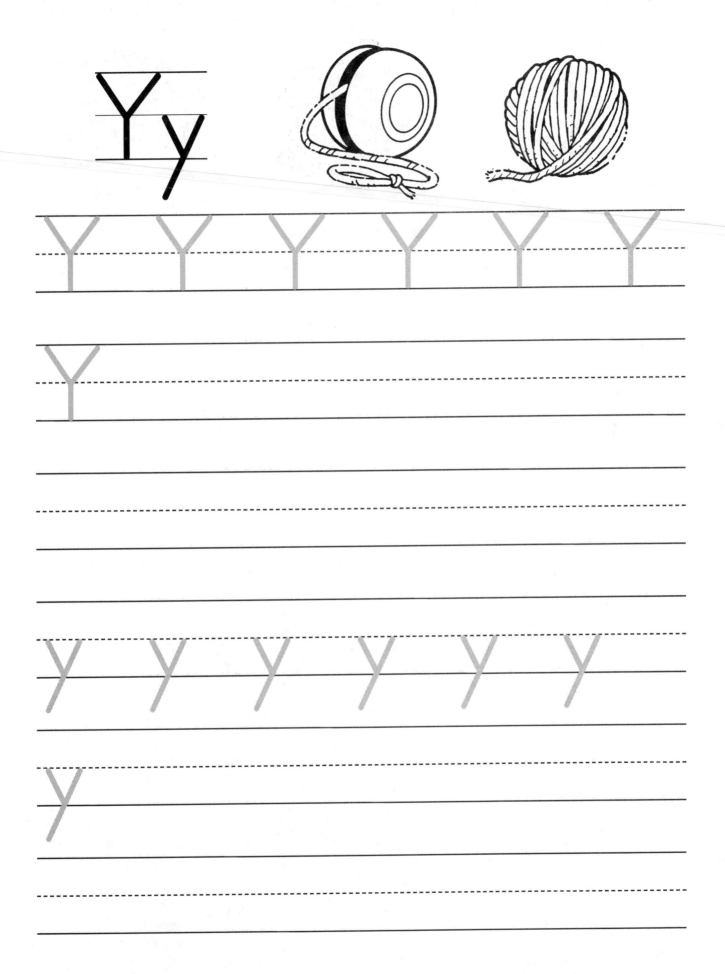

Ascenders

Descenders

g

j

p

q

y

g j p q y

Consonant Combinations

bl bl

block

fl fl

flag

sl sl

sled

Consonant Combinations *(cont.)*

dr dr

dress

fr fr

frog

gr gr

grapes

Consonant Combinations *(cont.)*

sh sh

sheep

sk sk

skunk

sn sn

snake

Consonant Combinations *(cont.)*

sch   sch

school

scr   scr

screw

str   str

street

Consonant Combinations (cont.)

th   th

thumb

tr   tr

tree

tw   tw

twig

Consonant Combinations *(cont.)*

ck   ck

lock

mp   mp

lamp

nk   nk

ink

Vowel Combinations

ai ai

pail

io io

lion

ay ay

hay

Vowel Combinations *(cont.)*

ea   ea

seal

ee   ee

deer

ie   ie

pie

Vowel Combinations *(cont.)*

oa oa

boat

ou ou

mouse

ea ea

read

Vowel Combinations *(cont.)*

ue   ue

glue

ui   ui

fruit

uu   uu

vacuum

Numbers and Number Words

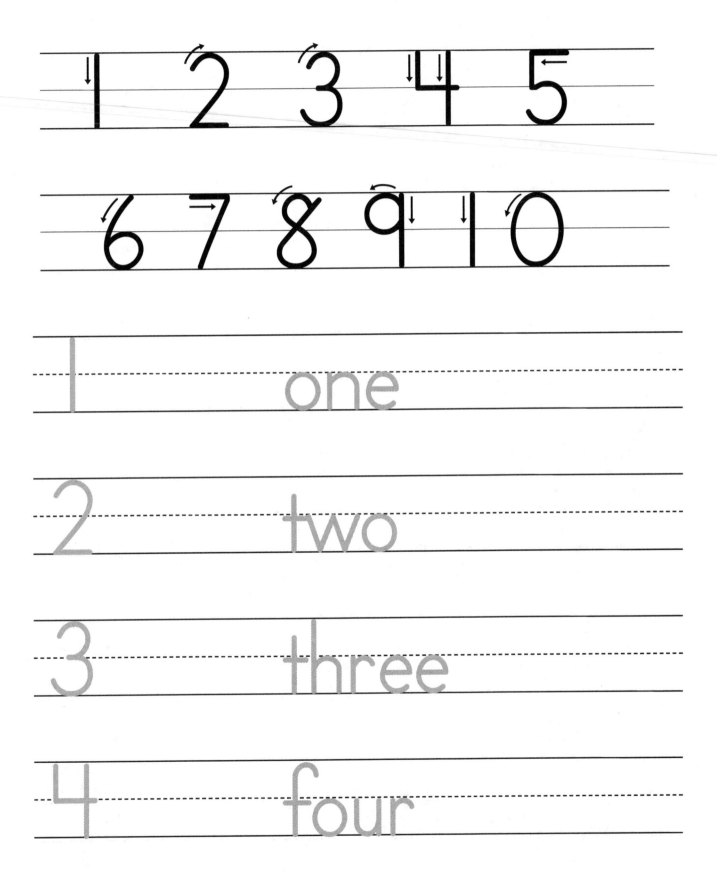

Numbers and Number Words (cont.)

5   five

6   six

7   seven

8   eight

9   nine

10   ten

Color Words

red

blue

yellow

green

orange

brown

Practice Page